DOWNSIDE OF DRUGS

Alcohol & Tobacco

DOWNSIDE of DRUGS

ADHD Medication Abuse: Ritalin®, Adderall®, & Other Addictive Stimulants

Alcohol & Tobacco

Caffeine: Energy Drinks, Coffee, Soda, & Pills

Dangerous Depressants & Sedatives

Doping: Human Growth Hormone, Steroids, & Other Performance-Enhancing Drugs

Hard Drugs: Cocaine, LSD, PCP, & Heroin

Marijuana: Legal & Developmental Consequences

Methamphetamine & Other Amphetamines

New Drugs: Bath Salts, Spice, Salvia, & Designer Drugs

Over-the-Counter Medications

Prescription Painkillers: OxyContin®, Percocet®, Vicodin®, & Other Addictive Analgesics

DOWNSIDE OF DRUGS

Alcohol & Tobacco

Rosa Waters

Mason Crest

Mason Crest
450 Parkway Drive, Suite D
Broomall, PA 19008
www.masoncrest.com

Printed and bound in the United States of America.

First printing
9 8 7 6 5 4 3 2 1

Series ISBN: 978-1-4222-3015-2
Hardcover ISBN: 978-1-4222-3017-6
Paperback ISBN: 978-1-4222-3190-6
ebook ISBN: 978-1-4222-8803-0

Cataloging-in-Publication Data on file with the Library of Congress.

Contents

INTRODUCTION

One of the best parts of getting older is the opportunity to make your own choices. As your parents give you more space and you spend more time with friends than family, you are called upon to make more decisions for yourself. Many important decisions that present themselves in the teen years may change your life. The people with whom you are friendly, how much effort you put into school and other activities, and what kinds of experiences you choose for yourself all affect the person you will become as you emerge from being a child into becoming a young adult.

One of the most important decisions you will make is whether or not you use substances like alcohol, marijuana, crystal meth, and cocaine. Even using prescription medicines incorrectly or relying on caffeine to get through your daily life can shape your life today and your future tomorrow. These decisions can impact all the other decisions you make. If you decide to say yes to drug abuse, the impact on your life is usually not a good one!

One suggestion I make to many of my patients is this: think about how you will respond to an offer to use drugs before it happens. In the heat of the moment, particularly if you're feeling some peer pressure, it can be hard to think clearly—so be prepared ahead of time. Thinking about why you don't want to use drugs and how you'll respond if you are asked to use them can make it easier to make a healthy decision when the time comes. Just like practicing a sport makes it easier to play in a big game, having thought about why drugs aren't a good fit for you and exactly what you might say to avoid them can give you the "practice" you need to do what's best for you. It can make a tough situation simpler once it arises.

In addition, talk about drugs with your parents or a trusted adult. This will both give you support and help you clarify your thinking. The decision is still yours to make, but adults can be a good resource. Take advantage of the information and help they can offer you.

Sometimes, young people fall into abusing drugs without really thinking about it ahead of time. It can sometimes be hard to recognize when you're making a decision that might hurt you. You might be with a friend or acquaintance in a situation that feels comfortable. There may be things in your life that are hard, and it could seem like using drugs might make them easier. It's also natural to be curious about new experiences. However, by not making a decision ahead of time, you may be actually making a decision without realizing it, one that will limit your choices in the future.

When someone offers you drugs, there is no flashing sign that says, "Hey, think about what you're doing!" Making a good decision may be harder because the "fun" part happens immediately while the downside—the damage to your brain and the rest of your body—may not be obvious right away. One of the biggest downsides of drugs is that they have long-term effects on your life. They could reduce your educational, career, and relationship opportunities. Drug use often leaves users with more problems than when they started.

Whenever you make a decision, it's important to know all the facts. When it comes to drugs, you'll need answers to questions like these: How do different drugs work? Is there any "safe" way to use drugs? How will drugs hurt my body and my brain? If I don't notice any bad effects right away, does that mean these drugs are safe? Are these drugs addictive? What are the legal consequences of using drugs? This book discusses these questions and helps give you the facts to make good decisions.

Reading this book is a great way to start, but if you still have questions, keep looking for the answers. There is a lot of information on the Internet, but not all of it is reliable. At the back of this book, you'll find a list of more books and good websites for finding out more about this drug. A good website is teens.drugabuse.gov, a site compiled for teens by the National Institute on Drug Abuse (NIDA). This is a reputable federal government agency that researches substance use and how to prevent it. This website does a good job looking at a lot of data and consolidating it into easy-to-understand messages.

What if you are worried you already have a problem with drugs? If that's the case, the best thing to do is talk to your doctor or another trusted adult to help figure out what to do next. They can help you find a place to get treatment.

Drugs have a downside—but as a young adult, you have the power to make decisions for yourself about what's best for you. Use your power wisely!

—*Joshua Borus, MD*

1. WHAT IS ALCOHOL?

You probably know that alcohol is a liquid that can make people drunk. But you may not know what alcohol really is. It's actually a chemical called ethanol that's a clear liquid when it's at room temperature. It's usually made by *fermenting* fruit or grain. People can't drink pure ethanol. If they did, they would die.

WHAT IS TOBACCO?

Tobacco is a green, leafy plant that is grown in warm climates. After it is picked, it is dried, ground up, and used in different ways.

Tobacco has a long history. More than a thousand years ago, the people who lived in Mexico carved drawings in stone showing tobacco use. In North America, Native people smoked tobacco through a pipe for special religious and medical purposes. They did not smoke every day. When Europeans arrived in North America, the Native people introduced them to tobacco.

Nicotine is one of the more than 4,000 chemicals in cigarettes. It is the chemical that makes tobacco habit forming.

For hundreds of years, people didn't know that tobacco could be dangerous. Then, in 1964, the U.S. Surgeon General wrote a report that said tobacco could cause cancer. Since then, more and more laws have been passed in the United States and around the world to try to control the use and production of tobacco products.

SURGEON GENERAL'S WARNING: Smoking Causes Lung Cancer, Heart Disease, Emphysema, And May Complicate Pregnancy

2. WHAT ARE THE DOWNSIDES OF USING ALCOHOL AND TOBACCO?

Alcohol and tobacco are both substances that when they are *ingested* change the body in some way. This makes them both drugs. Drugs change the way our bodies work. They can change the way we feel. Many people like the way alcohol and tobacco make them feel. But alcohol and tobacco have a downside!

Drugs can do good things, like cure diseases and take away pain. Drugs can also damage our bodies, especially when they're abused. When alcohol and tobacco are *abused* they can both seriously damage our bodies. They can even kill us.

Alcohol abuse results in 2.5 million deaths each year. Around the world, 320,000 young people between the age of 15 and 29 die from alcohol-related causes every year.

Smoking killed 100 million people in the 20th century, and is predicted to kill 1 billion in the 21st century. Half of all smokers will die early unless they stop smoking.

Alcohol and tobacco can also give us other problems in life. They are *addictive*. They can get in the way of our studies and work. They can hurt our relationships with friends and family. And they are expensive. If you smoke 4 cigarettes a day for the next 10 years, you'll have spent almost $4,000. If you smoke a pack a day, you'll have spent more than $18,000. If you drink only 2 days a week and have only 4 drinks each day, you'll end up spending about $2,000 a year on alcohol. In 10 years, that comes to about $20,000. You could pay for a pretty nice car with either of those amounts of money!

3. WHAT ARE THE LEGAL CONSEQUENCES OF USING ALCOHOL AND TOBACCO FOR YOUNG PEOPLE?

States have various laws that *prohibit* teens under 18 from buying, using, or possessing tobacco products. It's against the law!

In the United States, you must be 21 before you can buy or drink alcoholic beverages. It is against the law for anyone to sell or give alcoholic beverages to you or to let you drink with him or her in a bar or a store.

If you borrow a driver's license or change the age on yours to show that you are over 21, you are also breaking the law. Any person who gives a false ID to you is committing a crime too. You cannot lend, borrow, or alter a driver's license or other ID in any way.

4. HOW DO PEOPLE USE TOBACCO?

Tobacco can be smoked in a cigarette, in a pipe, or in a cigar. It can be chewed (called smokeless tobacco or chewing tobacco) or sniffed through the nose (called snuff). All forms of tobacco have health hazards.

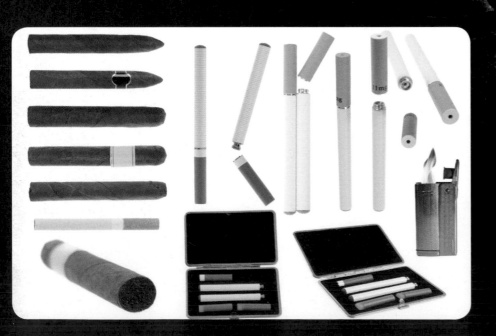

HOW DO PEOPLE USE ALCOHOL?

Alcohol comes in various forms. People drink it with meals. They drink it to celebrate. They drink it at bars and at parties. For adults, *moderate* alcohol *consumption* is not usually dangerous, but alcohol abuse at any age can be deadly.

Different kinds of alcoholic drinks have different amounts of alcohol (ethanol) in them.

Beer = 4 to 6 % alcohol
Wine = 7 to 15 % alcohol
Champagne = 8 to 14 % alcohol
Distilled spirits (rum, gin, vodka, whiskey, for example) = 40 to 95 % alcohol

17

5. WHAT DOES ALCOHOL DO ONCE IT'S INSIDE YOUR BODY?

The body responds to alcohol in stages. The more alcohol you have in your blood (blood alcohol content or BAC), the greater the effect on your body. As alcohol affects different parts of your body, your behavior will change too.

As a rule of thumb, an average person can get rid of about a half ounce (15 ml) of alcohol per hour. So it would take approximately one hour for your body to get rid of the alcohol from a 12-ounce (355 ml) can of beer. BAC increases when the body absorbs alcohol faster than it can get rid of it. Because the body can only get rid of about one drink per hour, drinking several drinks in an hour will increase your BAC much more than having one drink over a period of an hour or more.

BAC = 0.03 to 0.12 percent

People become more self-confident or daring, so they take risks they might not otherwise take. Their attention span shortens. Their judgment is not as good.

BAC = 0.09 to 0.25 percent

People become sleepy. They have trouble understanding or remembering things. They do not react to situations as quickly. They begin to lose their balance easily. Their vision becomes blurry.

BAC = 0.18 to 0.30 percent

People are confused. They cannot see clearly. They are sleepy. They have slurred speech. They are clumsy. They may not feel pain as much as a sober person would.

BAC = 0.25 to 0.4 percent

People can barely move at all. They cannot stand or walk. They may vomit. They may go in and out of consciousness.

BAC = 0.35 to 0.50 percent

People are unconscious. Their breathing is slower and more shallow. Their heart rate may slow. They may die.

BAC more than 0.50 percent

People usually stop breathing and die.

6. WHAT DOES TOBACCO DO ONCE IT'S INSIDE YOUR BODY?

Nicotine, the chemical in tobacco that acts as a drug, is a stimulant. That means it speeds up the nervous system, so it makes you feel like you have more energy. It makes the heart beat faster and raises blood pressure because it narrows the blood vessels. All this can put a strain on the heart. Smoking causes a lack of oxygen and shortness of breath.

Teenagers who smoke have more trouble sleeping than those who do not smoke.

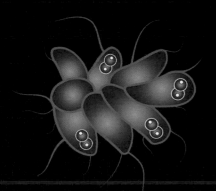

Teens who smoke produce twice as much **phlegm** as teens who don't.

Smokers run slower and can't run as far as nonsmokers.

Teens who smoke break out more than those who don't— and their zits last longer.

Teens who smoke are more likely to catch a cold than those who don't, and their symptoms will probably be worse and last longer.

Teenagers who smoke use more medications than those who do not smoke.

7. HOW DOES ALCOHOL CHANGE YOUR BRAIN?

Alcohol acts on the nerve cells within the brain. It interferes with communication between nerve cells, as well as between nerve cells and all the other cells in your body. This is why alcohol makes it hard for people to think and why it makes people clumsy.

Long-term drinking can leave permanent damage, causing the brain to shrink. It can also cause a condition called Wernicke-Korsakoff syndrome. People with Wernicke-Korsakoff syndrome are confused and clumsy. They may also have memory and learning problems.

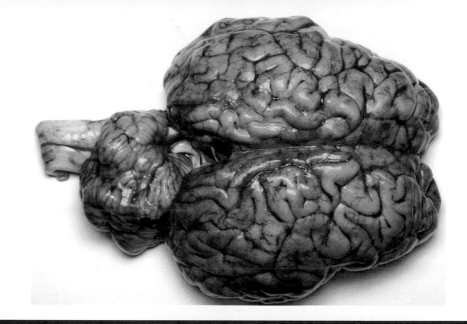

Frontal Lobe
Parietal Lobe
Temporal Lobe
Occipital Lobe
Cerebellum
Brain Stem

STRUCTURE OF THE HUMAN BRAIN

Alcohol affects various parts of the brain. The parts of your brain that control thinking and judgment are affected first. As BAC increases, more and more parts of the brain are affected. When BAC gets high enough, the parts of your brain that control your autonomic functions, like breathing and your heartbeat, will also shut down.

Long-term drinking can also change the chemicals in the brain. The brain's cells depend on alcohol, so when the person stops or cuts down her drinking, within 24 to 72 hours the brain goes into what is known as withdrawal. Symptoms of withdrawal include **disorientation**, **hallucinations**, **delirium tremens (DTs)**, nausea, sweating, and **seizures**.

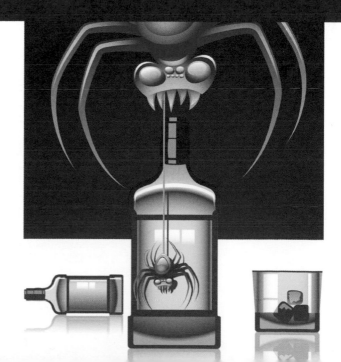

8. WHAT DOES TOBACCO SMOKE DO TO YOUR LUNGS?

Besides nicotine, the chemical that turns tobacco into a drug, tobacco smoke also contains thousands of other chemicals. When a smoker breathes in these chemicals, they irritate the lungs' cells. After a while, they start to damage the lungs. Eventually, they can cause cancer, a disease where the cells in the lungs start to grow too fast. Each year, many people die from lung cancer caused by tobacco.

If you're a man and you smoke, you're 23 times more likely to get lung cancer than someone who doesn't smoke. If you're a woman and you smoke, you're 18 times more likely to get lung cancer.

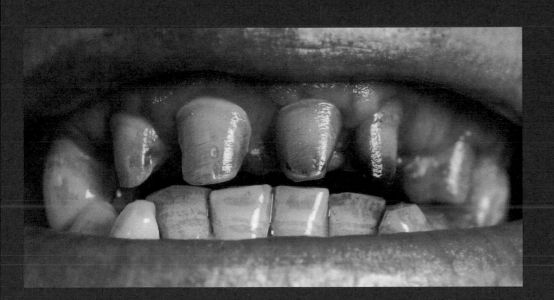

Tar is the sticky brown substance in cigarette smoke. It stains your teeth and fingernails. And it not only makes your teeth brown and ugly; it also stains the inside of your lungs.

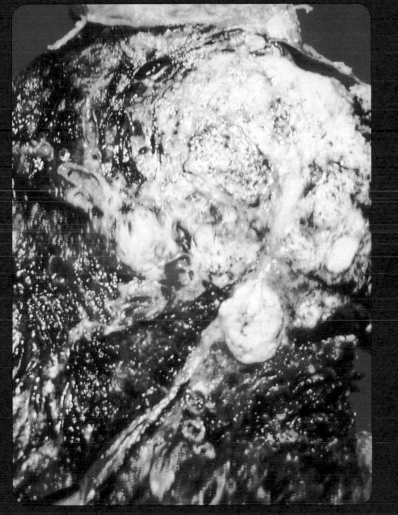

Hydrogen cyanide is another chemical in tobacco smoke. The lungs have tiny hairs that help to clean the lungs by moving out dust and dirt. Hydrogen cyanide stops these tiny hairs from working properly. This means the poisonous chemicals in tobacco smoke can build up inside the lungs, causing the lung tissue to look like the diseased lung shown here.

Tobacco smoke contains dangerous metals, including arsenic, cadmium and lead. Several of these metals cause cancer. They can turn a healthy lung, like the one shown here on the left, into a sick lung like the one on the right.

9. WHAT DOES TOBACCO DO TO YOUR HEART?

Smoking causes heart disease. In fact, 30 percent of all heart disease deaths are caused by cigarette smoking.

People who smoke have a 2 to 4 times higher chance of having heart disease. And smokers continue to increase their risk of heart attack the longer they smoke.

The nicotine in cigarette smoke causes heart disease by

- decreasing oxygen to your heart.
- increasing blood pressure and heart rate.
- increasing blood *clotting*.
- damaging the cells that line the arteries in your heart and other blood vessels.

Cigarette smoke contains carbon monoxide. It's an odorless gas that in large doses can kill you because it takes the place of oxygen in the blood. This means that less oxygen reaches the heart.

10. WHAT ELSE CAN TOBACCO DO TO YOUR BODY?

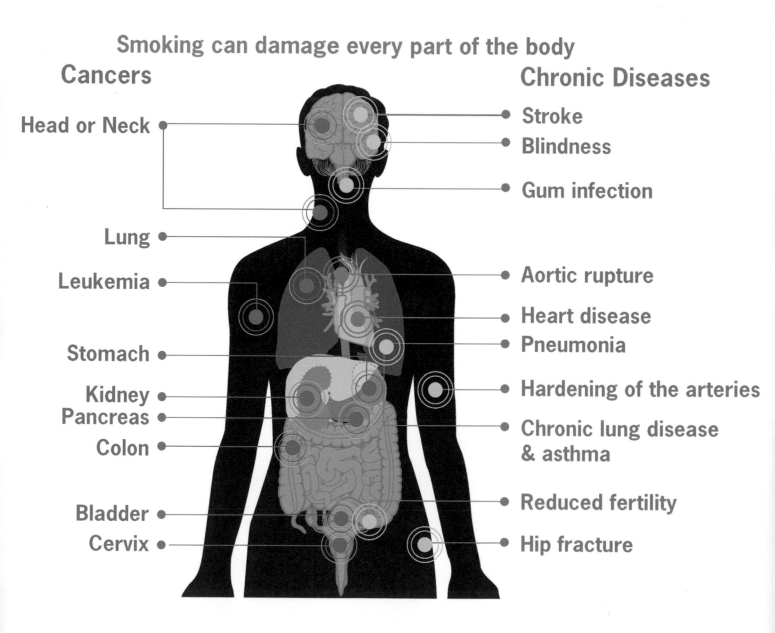

Smoking can damage every part of the body

Cancers

- Head or Neck
- Lung
- Leukemia
- Stomach
- Kidney
- Pancreas
- Colon
- Bladder
- Cervix

Chronic Diseases

- Stroke
- Blindness
- Gum infection
- Aortic rupture
- Heart disease
- Pneumonia
- Hardening of the arteries
- Chronic lung disease & asthma
- Reduced fertility
- Hip fracture

Your risk of certain other types of cancer besides lung cancer increases if you use chewing tobacco or other types of smokeless tobacco. You could get cancer of your *esophagus*, as well as cancers of your mouth, throat, cheek, gums, lips, and tongue. Mouth cancer is ugly!

WARNING: This product can cause mouth cancer

Chewing tobacco and other forms of smokeless tobacco cause tooth decay. That's because chewing tobacco contains high amounts of sugar, which causes cavities. Chewing tobacco also contains coarse particles that can irritate your gums and scratch away at the enamel on your teeth, making places where germs can get it and cause cavities.

The sugar and irritants in chewing tobacco and other forms of smokeless tobacco can make your gums pull away from your teeth. Over time you can develop gum disease. Your teeth may fall out.

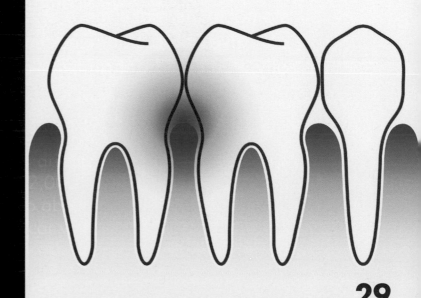

11. HOW CAN ALCOHOL DAMAGE YOUR BODY?

Alcohol can damage your brain, but it can also hurt other parts of your body too.

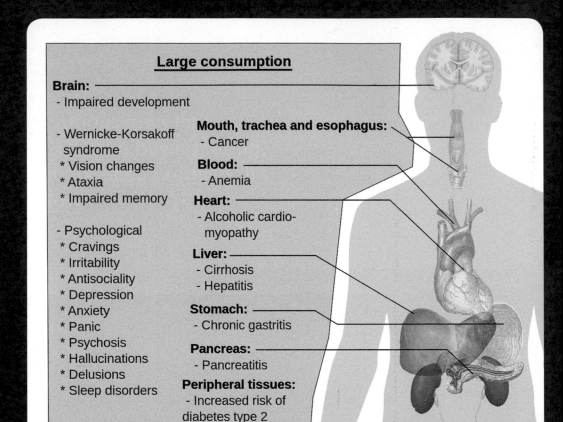

Large consumption

Brain:
- Impaired development

- Wernicke-Korsakoff syndrome
* Vision changes
* Ataxia
* Impaired memory

- Psychological
* Cravings
* Irritability
* Antisociality
* Depression
* Anxiety
* Panic
* Psychosis
* Hallucinations
* Delusions
* Sleep disorders

Mouth, trachea and esophagus:
- Cancer

Blood:
- Anemia

Heart:
- Alcoholic cardio-myopathy

Liver:
- Cirrhosis
- Hepatitis

Stomach:
- Chronic gastritis

Pancreas:
- Pancreatitis

Peripheral tissues:
- Increased risk of diabetes type 2

Too much alcohol can make you throw up. Alcohol irritates the linings of your stomach and intestines. Your stomach will make more acid, which can give you a stomachache. Eventually, you could get an ulcer or cancer.

Alcohol reduces blood flow to muscles. This can make your muscles ache.

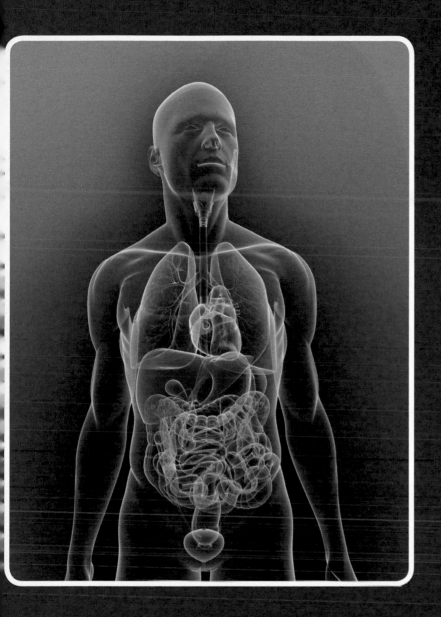

Your liver is the organ that helps your body get alcohol out of your system. The liver has to work harder than it would normally when you drink alcohol. Eventually, too much alcohol will damage your liver. The liver's cells will start to die. It will no longer be able to do its job, which will make you very sick. Eventually, it could kill you.

Long-term alcohol use causes high blood pressure. This can lead to *stroke*.

Males who drink a lot of alcohol make fewer sperm.

12. WHY IS ALCOHOL ADDICTIVE?

When a person is addicted to something, she cannot control how often she uses it. She depends on it to help her cope with daily life. Her body needs it in order to function.

Scientists have discovered that one of the things that makes alcohol so addictive is that it changes brain chemicals. It makes the brain release chemicals that cause pleasure and satisfaction. The more a person drinks, the more her brain depends on alcohol to produce these feelings. After a while, it's very hard for her to feel pleasure and satisfaction from all the other things in life that normally make us feel happy. Instead, if she wants to feel good, she needs to drink. And the longer she's been drinking, the more alcohol she'll need to get those good feelings.

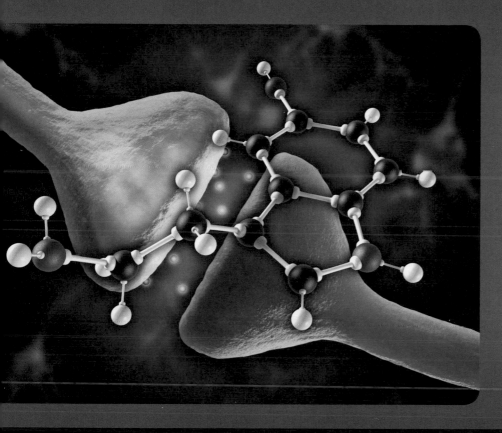

Alcohol makes the brain produce endorphins. These are chemicals that change the way nerve cells pass messages. Lots of things besides alcohol trigger our brains to make endorphins. Our favorite foods, sex, and exercise are all things that can produce the rush of happy feeling that endorphins give us. Brains that are dependent on alcohol for endorphins, though, don't enjoy these other things as much.

Alcohol also triggers dopamine production in the brain. Dopamine is another neurotransmitter (a chemical that help nerves pass messages), and like endorphins, it's connected to good feelings. Dopamine controls the brain's reward and pleasure centers. It helps our brains see good things that we want and then take action to get them. When our brains have learned to depend on alcohol, though, we're not able to see all the other good things in life.

When someone who is an alcoholic (addicted to alcohol) tries to quit drinking, he goes through withdrawal. He'll feel shaky and sweaty and sick to his stomach.

13. WHY IS TOBACCO ADDICTIVE?

Each time you puff on a cigarette, you're sucking nicotine into your lungs, where it is absorbed into your blood. It only takes 8 seconds for nicotine to hit your brain. Once it's there, it changes the way brain cells communicate with each other.

Nicotine, like alcohol, makes your brain release dopamine. This is why people who smoke feel good when they light up. However, the effect wears off fast, so people who smoke get the urge to light up again for another shot of dopamine. Nicotine is one of the chemicals in tobacco that make it addictive. It's what makes some people turn into "chain smokers," lighting up a new cigarette as soon as the last one is smoked.

Acetaldehyde, another chemical in tobacco smoke, heightens the feelings of pleasure that nicotine produces. **Researchers** have found that this is particularly true in adolescent brains. This may be one reason why teenagers are more likely to become addicted to tobacco than adults are.

When people quit smoking, they usually experience withdrawal symptoms. Nicotine withdrawal symptoms include *irritability*, problems with thinking and paying attention, sleep disturbances, increased appetite, and craving. Craving—an intense urge for nicotine that can last for six months or longer—makes quitting hard.

14. HOW DOES USING ALCOHOL OR TOBACCO CHANGE THE WAY YOU DO IN SCHOOL?

Using alcohol and tobacco can make you less healthy—and when you're not as healthy, you don't learn as well. You have problems focusing on your classes and homework. You don't remember things as easily. You're also more likely to miss school because you don't feel well.

Researchers have found that alcohol problems are tied to lower grades, poor school attendance, and increases in dropout rates. And 52% of all high school students who average Ds and Fs on their schoolwork smoke cigarettes or use other tobacco products—but only 16% of A students use tobacco.

High school students who miss 10 or more days of school a month are 64% more likely to be smokers.

Middle school students who don't use alcohol score higher on reading and math tests than students who do.

Among high school students, those who use alcohol are five times more likely to drop out than those who don't use alcohol.

15. WHY IS DRINKING AND DRIVING SO DANGEROUS?

When you're driving, you need to be alert so you can pay close attention to the road. You need to be able to see well. You need to be able to react quickly if something unexpected happens.

Now look back at page 19. See how only a little alcohol in your blood affects you? Alcohol makes you drowsy. If you've been drinking, you can't concentrate, your eyes are blurry, you're less coordinated than usual, and your reaction time is slower. Alcohol and driving make a terrible combination! If you drink and drive, it's only a question of time before you'll have an accident.

Every day in the United States, another 27 people die because of drunk driving.

One out of every three people will be in an accident caused by a drunk driver at some point in their lives.

Alcohol *impairs* your judgment. Speeding can seem like a good idea when you're drunk—when actually, because your coordination and reaction time are lower than usual, you're less able to handle a speeding vehicle than you would be normally.

Every year in the United States alone, more than 10,000 people die and more than 300,000 are injured in accidents caused by drunk driving.

All U.S. states have made a BAC of .08% as the legal limit for operating a motor vehicle for drivers who are 21 years or older. If you're under 21, however, it's against the law for you to drive with ANY alcohol in your blood. Police can tell how much alcohol you have in your blood by testing your breath. If you're caught drinking and driving, you'll be arrested.

If you know you're going to be drinking, be sure to have a designated driver, someone who will drive you home—and keep you and everyone else on the road safe.

16. MORE QUESTIONS?

How dangerous is drinking alcohol? Doesn't everyone do it?

There are roughly 80,000 deaths in the United States alone that are related to alcohol abuse every year, making it the third highest cause of death in the United States.

How do I know if I have a problem with alcohol?

Answer the following questions honestly. The more times you answer yes, the more like it is that you have a drinking problem.

- Do you miss school because you've been drinking?
- Do you get in fights with your friends and family because you've been drinking?
- Do you "binge drink" (have 5 or more drinks in a row if you're a guy, 4 or more drinks in a row if you're a girl)?
- Do you drink because you're unhappy?
- Have you tried to quit drinking and not been able to?
- Do you ever drink so much that you black out?
- Do you often drink more than you meant to?

How can I stop drinking?

If you're ready to admit you have a drinking problem, you've already taken a big first step. It takes a lot of courage to face alcohol abuse head on. Your next step is to ask for help. Because alcohol is addictive, it's very hard to stop drinking all by yourself. You'll need support from your friends and family. Talk to your doctor, your school counselor, or another adult you trust. They'll be able to help you decide what you should do next.

How can I quit smoking?

When you make up your mind to quit smoking, be prepared that it will be hard. If you're addicted to cigarettes or another tobacco product, your body craves nicotine. But you can do it! Set a start date for quitting. Put it in writing. Tell your friends and ask them to support you (tell your family too, if they know you smoke). When your start date for quitting arrives, throw away your cigarettes. If you think you need extra help, talk to your doctor about medications she can prescribe that will help make quitting easier.

FIND OUT MORE IN BOOKS

Carlson, Hannah. *Addiction: The Brain Disease.* Branford, Conn.: Bick, 2010.

Chastain, Zachary. *Tobacco: Through the Smoke Screen.* Broomall, Pa.: Mason Crest, 2012.

Esherick, Joan. *Smoking-Related Health Issues.* Broomall, Pa.: Mason Crest, 2013.

Espejo, Roman. *Alcohol.* Farmington Hills, Mich.: Greenhaven Press, 2012.

Hyde, Margaret. *Smoking 101.* Minneapolis, Minn.: Twenty-First Century Books, 2005.

Kuhn, Cynthia. *Buzzed: The Straight Facts About the Most Used and Abused Drugs from Alcohol to Ecstasy.* New York: Norton, 2008.

Paris, Stephanie. *Straight Talk: Drugs and Alcohol.* Westminster, Calif.: Teacher Created Materials, 2013.

Synder, Gail. *Teens and Alcohol.* Broomall, Pa.: Mason Crest, 2008.

Wand, Kelly. *Smoking and Tobacco.* Farmington Hills, Mich.: Greenhaven Press, 2012.

FIND OUT MORE ON THE INTERNET

Alcohol: Thinking About Drinking
pbskids.org/itsmylife/body/alcohol

Binge Drinking
kidshealth.org/teen/drug_alcohol/alcohol/binge_drink.html#cat20139

Brain and Addiction
teens.drugabuse.gov/drug-facts/brain-and-addiction

Drug Facts: Tobacco
teens.drugabuse.gov/drug-facts/tobacco

Facts About Teens and Alcohol
www.dosomething.org/tipsandtools/11-facts-about-teens-and-alcohol

The Facts on Drunk Driving
www.kidzworld.com/article/9591-the-facts-on-drunk-driving

Smokeless Tobacco
kidshealth.org/teen/drug_alcohol/tobacco/smokeless.html#cat20138

Smoking and Asthma
kidshealth.org/teen/drug_alcohol/tobacco/smoking_asthma.html?tracking=T_Related-Article

Stop Smoking: Your Personal Plan
kidshealth.org/teen/your_body/take_care/smoking_plan.html?tracking=T_RelatedArticle

GLOSSARY

abused: Used a drug in a way that was harmful.

addictive: Causing dependence.

clotting: The process by which blood becomes thicker, to slow down bleeding.

delirium tremens (DTs): A disorder common in alcoholics, which includes trembling and hallucinations.

disorientation: A feeling of being confused or lost.

esophagus: The muscular tube that leads from your mouth down to your stomach.

fermenting: The process by which sugars, such as those in fruit juices, are converted to alcohol.

hallucinations: Things that you see and hear that aren't really there.

impairs: Damages your mental or physical abilities in some way.

ingested: Took into the body by swallowing.

irritability: A mood where you become easily annoyed or angry.

moderate: An average amount; not too much or too little.

phlegm: Mucus produced in your lungs and nose. Having lots of phlegm often means you are sick or unhealthy.

prohibit: Prevent; don't allow.

researchers: Scientists who work to make new discoveries.

seizures: Abnormal electrical activity in the brain that can cause muscle spasms and unconsciousness.

stroke: A burst or blocked blood vessel in your brain. This can cause brain damage.

ulcer: A sore on the inside of your stomach.

INDEX

PICTURE CREDITS

ABOUT THE AUTHOR
AND THE CONSULTANT

ROSA WATERS lives in New York State. She has worked as a writer for several years, producing works on health, history, and other topics.

DR. JOSHUA BORUS, MD, MPH, graduated from the Harvard Medical School and the Harvard School of Public Health. He completed a residency in pediatrics and then served as chief resident at Floating Hospital for Children at Tufts Medical Center before completing a fellowship in Adolescent Medicine at Boston Children's Hospital. He is currently an attending physician in the Division of Adolescent and Young Adult Medicine at Boston Children's Hospital and an instructor of pediatrics at Harvard Medical School.